T0052720

WORLD WINDOWS

# Solids, Liquids, and Gases

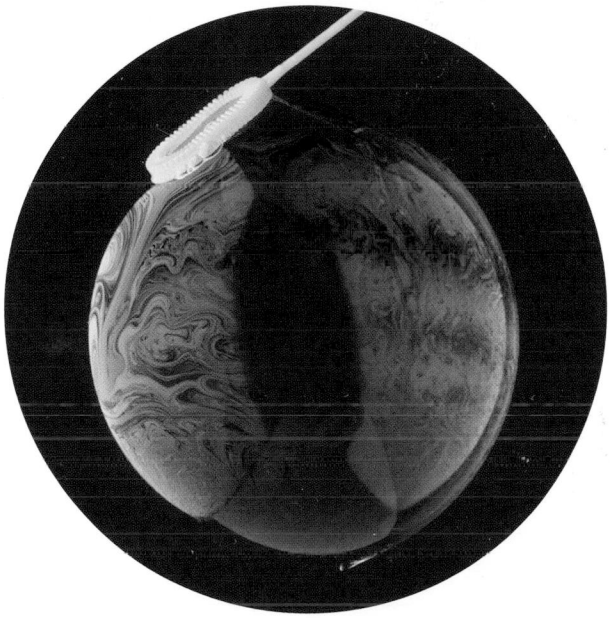

HEINLE CENGAGE Learning™

Y|S|G A YBM COMPANY Young & Son Global, Inc.

# What liquids do you drink?

# Contents


| | |
|---|---|
| Vocabulary | 4 |
| Matter | 6 |
| Solids | 8 |
| Liquids | 10 |
| Gases | 12 |
| Summary | 14 |
| Fun Facts | 15 |
| Glossary and Index | 16 |

# Vocabulary

gas
measure
mass

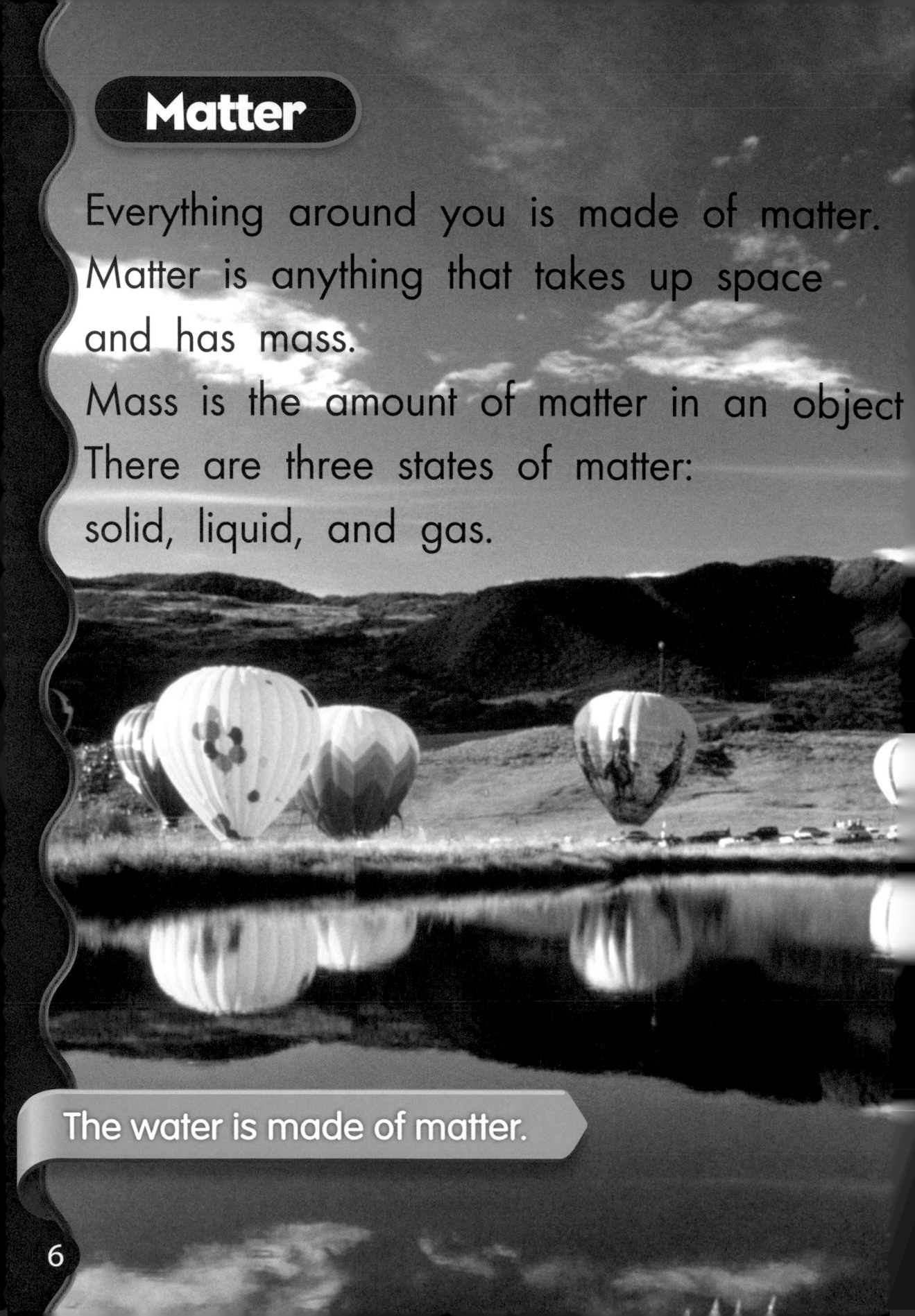

## Matter

Everything around you is made of matter. Matter is anything that takes up space and has mass.

Mass is the amount of matter in an object

There are three states of matter: solid, liquid, and gas.

The water is made of matter.

The air in the sky and inside the balloons is made of matter.

The grass is made of matter.

# Solids

A solid takes up space and has mass.
Only a solid has its own shape.
It does not change shape.
You can measure the mass of a solid with a balance.
Crayons, scissors, and books are all solids.

You can measure the length of a solid with a ruler.

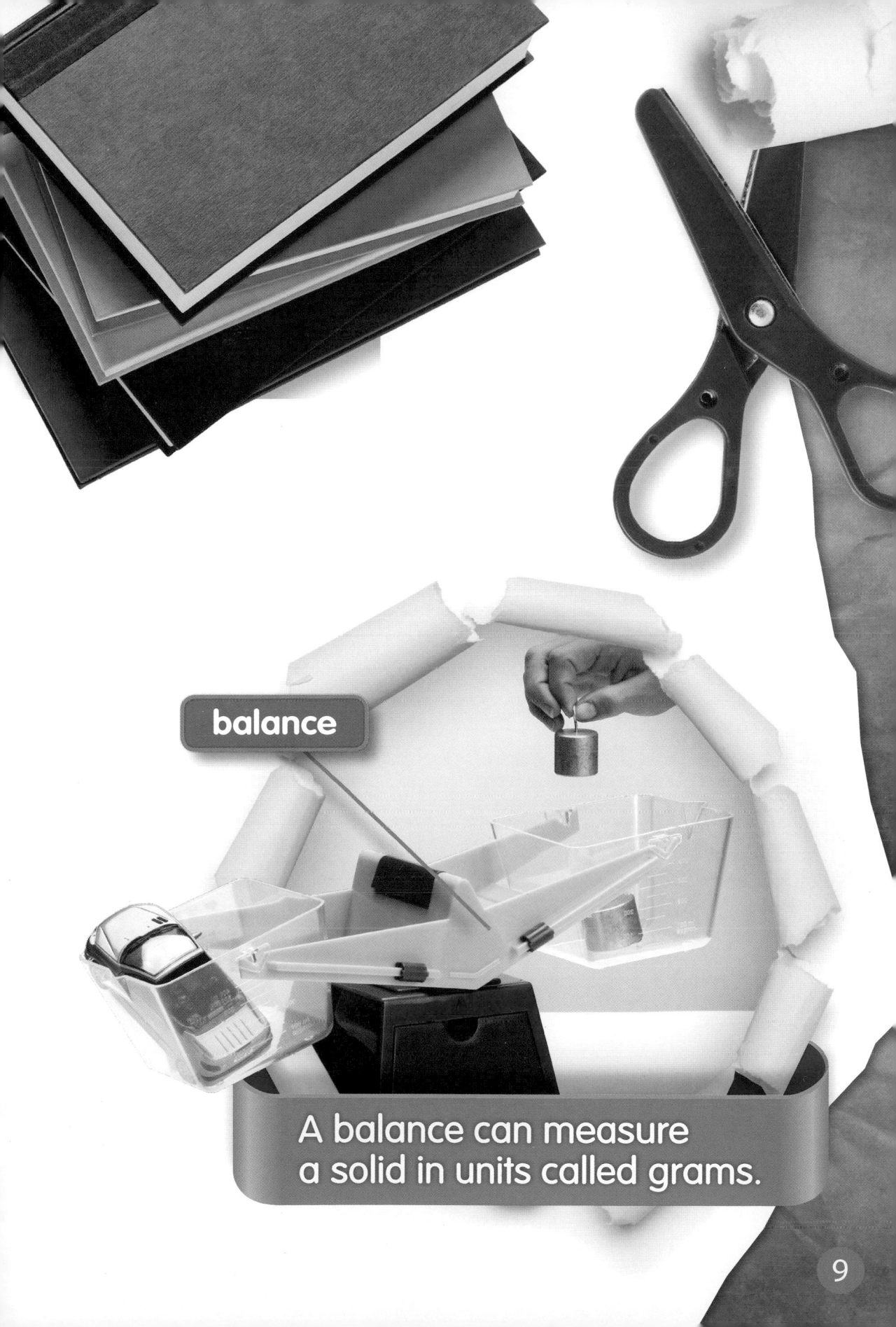


A balance can measure a solid in units called grams.

# Liquids

A liquid takes up space and has mass, too. Unlike a solid, it does not have its own shape. It takes the shape of its container. You can use a measuring cup to find out how much space a liquid takes up. Milk, juice, and water are all liquids.

Look at the different shapes a liquid can take.

A measuring cup can measure a liquid in units called milliliters.

# Gases

A gas also takes up space and has mass. Like a liquid, it does not have its own shape.

It spreads out to fill its container.

There are gases inside balls and balloons. Gases also make up the air you breathe.

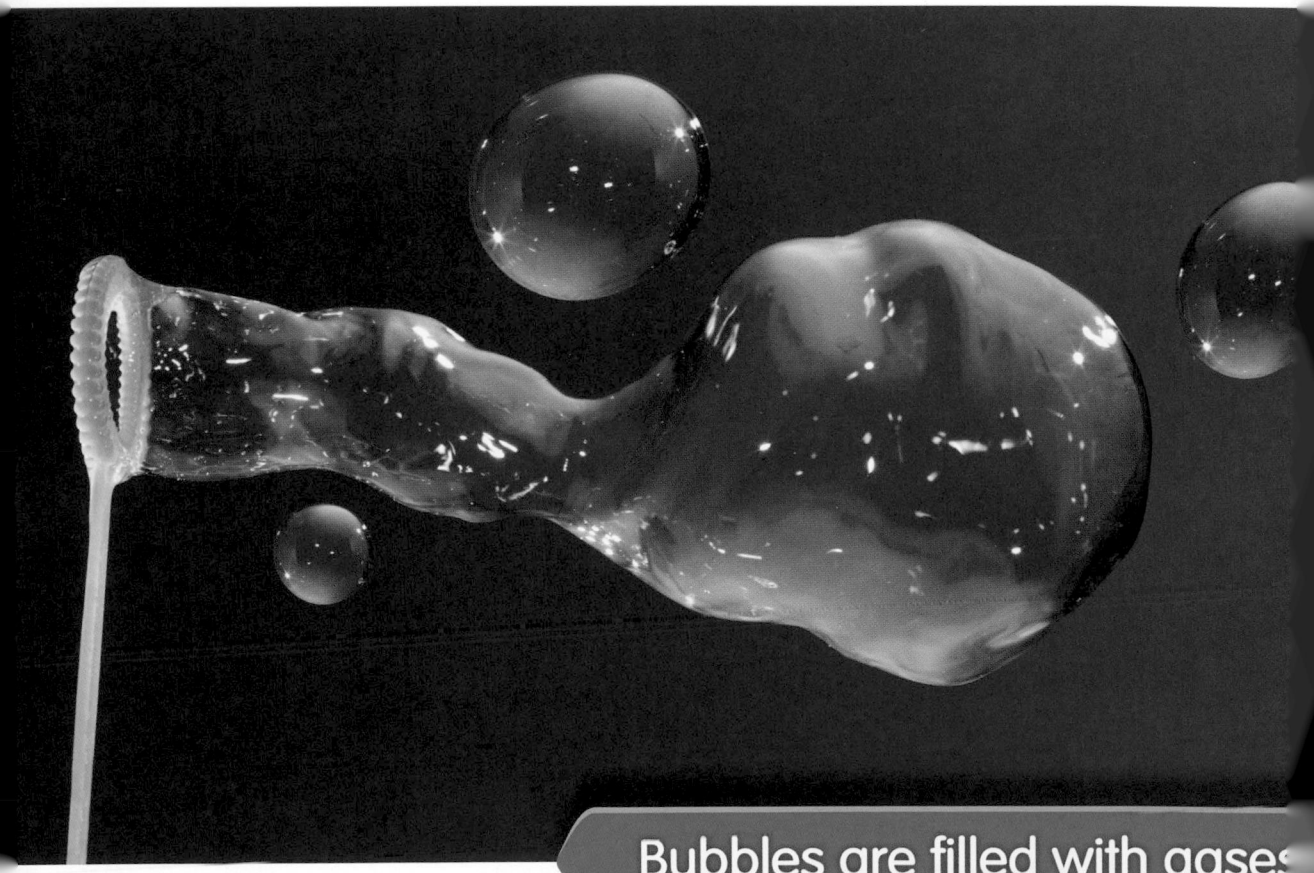

Bubbles are filled with gases

You cannot see air,
but you can feel it. How?

**Answers** : You can feel the wind!

## Summary

# What are these three states of matter? How are they different?

Fun Facts

# Water Can Change

The water we drink is a liquid. But cooling and heating can make water change into a solid and a gas, too!

When water freezes, it becomes ice. Ice is a solid. When water boils, it becomes steam. Steam is a gas. When steam cools, it forms tiny drops of water. The water is a liquid again.

## Glossary

**breathe**
To take air into and out of your lungs

**mass**
The amount of matter in an object

**measure**
To find out how long or how much something is

**shape**
The form of an object

**space**
An area that is empty or available

**spread**
To cover or open out over an area

**state**
The fact of being a liquid, solid, or gas

## Index


**balance,** 8–9
**container,** 10, 12
**gas,** 6, 12
**like,** 12
**liquid,** 6, 10–12
**mass,** 6, 8, 10, 12
**matter,** 6–7
**measure,** 8–9, 11
**shape,** 8, 10, 12
**solid,** 6, 8–10
**space,** 6, 8, 10, 12
**spreads,** 12
**takes up,** 6, 8, 10, 12
**unlike,** 10